Odysseys

FREEMAN PATTERSON

Odysseys

MEDITATIONS AND THOUGHTS
FOR A LIFE'S JOURNEY

A Phyllis Bruce Book
HarperCollins*PublishersLtd*

*For all my friends who share the journey, including those who travel
with me in memories and dreams*

I want to acknowledge the important contributions of Richard and Des Molyneux to the making of this book, and thank them for sharing their love of the Namib, and for their generosity and kindness to me over the years.

Also, I want to express my gratitude to De Beers Consolidated Mines Limited and, especially, to the management of Namdeb for providing access to the abandoned "diamond" towns located in restricted areas.

First edition

Canadian Cataloguing in Publication Data

Patterson, Freeman, 1937–
Odysseys : meditations and thoughts for a life's journey

"A Phyllis Bruce book."
ISBN 0-00-255765-7

1. Namib Desert (Namibia) — Pictorial works. 2. Ghost towns — Namibia — Pictorial works. 3. Landscape photography — Namibia. 4. Patterson, Freeman, 1937– . I. Title.

TR660.5.P37 1998   779'.36881'092   C98-931392-1

98 99 00 01 02 03 04 DWF 10 9 8 7 6 5 4 3 2 1

Printed and bound in Canada

Contents

Introduction / 1

Approaches / 8

Imprints / 15

Family / 24

Doors and Windows / 34

Metamorphoses / 45

Out of the Rubble / 56

Nature and Human Nature / 65

Cracks in the Walls / 72

Mortal Remains / 77

Departures / 85

Notes on Photographs / 89

There are simply no answers to some of the great pressing questions. You continue to live them out, making your life a worthy expression of a leaning into the light.

— Barry Lopez, *Arctic Dreams*

Introduction

The desert mining towns along the Atlantic coast of southern Namibia — Bogenfels, Pomona, Elizabeth Bay, and Kolmanskop — were built by German settlers in the early days of the twentieth century, long before I was born, and abandoned when the then economically exploitable deposits of diamonds were exhausted in the 1930s and early 1940s. The mine workers, managers, and their families no longer needed to live in this arid African land where rain seldom fell and supplying water was difficult and costly. So they left, taking their belongings and most of the furnishings from their homes, but leaving enough behind to provide rudimentary sketches of their lives. Then the entire area was sealed off, except to a later generation of workers and managers, and the region became in reality what it already was in name — Die Sperrgebiet, the Forbidden Territory.

The houses, the schools, the hospitals, and the clubs stood empty. There was no need to repair windows shattered by the driving force of wind and sand, no reason to shut doors that blew open and remained open as the sand piled against them. There was nobody to retrieve a discarded pair of gumboots, a bathtub, a bedstead, a piece of linoleum, or a barrel, artifacts that disappeared and reappeared on a schedule determined solely by the force and direction of the wind.

But the buildings didn't remain empty. They became the shelters and dens for black-backed jackals, hyenas, and other mammals, and the cool interiors welcomed insects and lured the lizards that follow them in search of food. Lichens began to nestle in the cracked and peeling paint, creating new wall tapestries and patterns on doors. Hardy desert shrubs gained a roothold where walls sheltered widening crevices in stone or concrete steps.

On my very first visit to one of these towns, the visual appearance of the buildings, long abandoned by the mothers, fathers, and children who lived, and worked, and played in them, filled me with emotions of sadness, longing, and desire. I felt that I was entering a dreamplace, and making pictures there would be a good way of remembering, of consciously retaining my experience, my dream — like writing it down — so I could endeavour later to understand its many meanings.

During the past few years, as I have presented these photographs in the form of "audiovisuals" and printed images to the public, I have come to realize that they evoke a more personal response from people of all ages than any other pictures I've made. It is because of your response that this book has been created. The thoughts and

reflections — meditations, perhaps — that accompany the photographs are also about feelings and ideas evoked by my visits to these incredible, dying towns. (To enable you to respond to the images in your own way, I have chosen to put my brief captions at the end of the book.)

Of course, I cannot remember the towns when they were newly built, when the interior walls of houses were freshly painted in vivid, saturated hues to provide visual relief and emotional distance from the hot sand, the protruding rocks, and the salty, grey mists that roll in quickly and unexpectedly from the Atlantic Ocean. I cannot recall the dinners and performances in the social clubs, nor women in long dresses bending their parasols toward the wind. I cannot remember the chatter of children excavating little treasures from the sand, nor their panic when a sandstorm or mist suddenly obliterated the rocks and dunes, markers that could guide them safely home. I cannot remember, because I was not there. These things I can only imagine.

However, these abandoned buildings, representations of a European culture that was stitched temporarily onto the African desert, function as icons that evoke the daily struggles with the sand, the thirst, the laughter, the tears, the reality of death, and the beauty of natural reclamation. The fact that there has been no restoration, except for a couple of buildings in Kolmanskop, perhaps explains why the towns are such potent symbols and, for many, such frightening ones — they have no successors.

For me the towns have reached the zenith of their symbolic power, and are more expressive now than they could ever have been when they were new, or if they had been restored.

I believe that they represent our collective, human story, which is, above all else, a nature story. Nature demands that we wander, that we lose our way, that we seek direction, that we develop and use our own physical and emotional resources in order to nurture our creative impulse. The sequential time periods or stages of life we employ in telling our story are, basically, illusions. There is one continuous journey for each of us, and each life story is a tale of transition. I have made and continue to make my own journeys through these towns and images, and each of you who finds meaning in them must do the same. I can travel with you, perhaps point out things you might have missed, but ultimately the journey you make will be yours alone.

Approaches

Where shall I begin? With my reaction to the distant view of a collection of abandoned buildings? Or with my subsequent feelings about a single artifact — perhaps a wine bottle protruding obliquely from the sand, or the potent symbol of a ragged curtain being sucked through a broken windowpane?

When I choose the overview, I miss most of the details. When I go closer to observe details, I lose sight of the whole. But is this visual limitation also an emotional or intellectual constraint? I don't need to see the surface details of an orange moon rising above a line of darkening dunes or snowy hills in the deepening blue twilight to experience a sense of wonder. On the other hand, the gentle touch of a lover's finger in the dark brings me a sense of the entire person and stimulates the full spectrum and intensity of my feelings. And poet William Blake wrote of seeing the world in a grain of sand. How apt in the Namib desert!

But every town is different from every other town, and every approach to a town is different from every other approach. Even when my feet are placed in footprints I made previously, and even if I stand there at precisely the same time as I did the day before, the angle of light will have altered slightly and the sky will be deeper blue or paler with dust. And I will be a day older. So every time I gaze upon the whole, it will be from a unique perspective. And each of my unique perspectives will be different from each of yours.

So how shall I begin? I will make a pragmatic decision based on the way things happened for me. I glimpsed each of the towns for the first time from a distance — perhaps as it suddenly emerged whole from behind a distant line of dunes, perhaps as it became the anticipated conclusion to a small series of visual clues, such as one building, then another, coming into view as my companions and I threaded our way through a range of sand-swept, rocky hills. I will begin with my approach to Bogenfels.

Six friends and I drove into Bogenfels from behind, as it were, so our first glimpse was of a single building. From out of nowhere, it seemed, the ruins of a once-grand house suddenly appeared on the near horizon. Despite the havoc wreaked by decades of exposure to wind-driven sand and salty drizzle, the house remains a commanding, arrogant presence, a "grande dame," the monarch of Bogenfels. From its elevated position on a rocky ridge, it stares down upon its subjects (a scattering of derelict houses that comes into view as you round the end of the ridge) with an air of regal superiority. In one visual sweep of Bogenfels, a person can ascertain the social structure of the community that once existed here.

On my first visit I was bothered by the system that, apparently, had deliberately woven social rank into the fabric of a community that never consisted of more than a few hundred souls. A hierarchical world may be necessary for practical reasons, but provides no excuse for valuing a manager above a worker, an adult above a child, or one ethnic group above another. Thomas Moore, a leading educator in the fields of archetypal psychology, mythology, and the imagination, put it as well as anybody when he wrote that we are not caring for the soul when we fabricate ways of denying its inferior stations.

Despite these thoughts and feelings, my initial response to Bogenfels was not at all unpleasant. Nature itself seemed to provide the levelling influence that I wanted. It may have been the grey, overcast sky and the spit of rain in the air that sucked the colour from the sand and the buildings, and painted the town in monochrome. It may have been that the grand house on the hilltop was more exposed to the elements and in a more advanced state of decay than some of the houses on the plain below. Whatever it was, I soon realized that, when the wind was up and the weather turned foul, whoever lived on the hill had more to worry about than those who lived below. The "perks" and trappings that come with being a monarch, which are often envied by the rest of us, are often little more than excess baggage.

Perhaps because Bogenfels is the smallest of the four towns, a mere way station in the desert really, perhaps because the buildings

are more widely separated than those in the other towns, perhaps because, when I first visited, the sky was darkly ominous when I arrived and remained that way for much of my stay, I felt lonely here, cut off from the rest of civilization, abandoned. Although there is a part of me that yearns to be alone in nature, there is another part of me, equally important, that craves the companionship of my fellow humans. In the Bogenfels of today, I felt I could die unnoticed.

And then, toward evening, the sun appeared! In a twinkling, my vision of life was altered, my funereal mood transformed into one of joyful excitement as the last of the sun's rays stroked the desert sands and marvellously illuminated the house on the hill. Where before I was walking, even wandering, now I had direction and momentum. I ran from spot to spot, eager to find uniquely new perspectives.

Later, as I trudged through the rapidly enveloping darkness toward the one building where it was still safe enough to toss a mattress and a sleeping bag on the floor, I contemplated the fact that all day long I had been relating a particular artifact — the grand house on the hill — to the entire town and the town to the artifact. And I thought of other situations, very different from this one, in which I have responded similarly — reflecting on the ways in which a sweep of wildflowers sets off a single blossom, for example, or, conversely, how the answer to a single question will confirm or destroy an entire argument or even a set of beliefs. Or how a simple, individual act of caring can heal a lifetime of wounds.

Imprints

One morning in Pomona I watched a black-backed jackal sniffing along the base of an old workshed. From where I stood I could see the footprints that another jackal had made recently, as it walked the length of the shed. There we were, two quite different mammals, using different senses and different signs to garner at least some of the same information. After "my" jackal had trotted off, I examined the tracks of the first jackal. Both animals were heading in the same direction and taking basically the same path. I followed them, making a third set of footprints in the sand. I doubt that any creature interpreted all these prints, but certainly none did once the wind began to obliterate the depressions. Some imprints have a very short existence.

Others, like Pomona itself, last much longer. The imprinting of the town on the desert will last longer, in fact has already lasted much longer, than its imprint on my memory. An imprint always requires a

receiver, a receptor. Every imprint disappears when the imprintee ceases to exist — the sand, my memory, even my willingness to receive.

Also, because of individual interests and experiences, we "receive" situations differently, and thus are imprinted in different ways. When a couple strolls through a summer meadow only one of them may remember individual blades or stalks of grass. In short, previous imprints affect the ways we register new ones.

At Kolmanskop, which is the only town open to the public, I am extremely conscious of the trails of footprints made by tourists. Fortunately, most visitors head straight for the largest buildings and, having "seen" them, retire to the little shop and café for a cappuccino, or clamber back into their vehicles and depart. However, they don't take their footprints with them. They cannot repair the sand patterns they have carelessly obliterated, and therefore are unable to readjust the sense of time and transition they have altered, or restore the feeling of loneliness they have destroyed. As for me, having learned how to move through the buildings like a ghost, I rejoice that the wind will surely rise again.

But a person can carry his sense of what is important to him, his imprinting, too far. On my second trip to the Forbidden Territory, I did just that. I was so engrossed in my exploration of the towns, especially Pomona, so single-minded in my pursuit of images that expressed the very deep feelings that the place evoked for me, that I became less than the best of company for the six friends with whom I

was travelling. They elected to spend the better part of each day exploring the surrounding desert, an extremely worthwhile and interesting project, and they left me in Pomona, where I wanted to be. Their days, on the whole, were more physically taxing than mine, and they looked forward to relaxing and having a good meal together in the camaraderie of the campfire. Unfortunately, I was unable to shift my focus easily and quickly, and sometimes I let it show.

Being the good people they are, they have forgiven and forgotten, but I haven't forgotten. Unconsciously, I was attempting to imprint them with my feelings, which was insensitive and ultimately futile. My emotional withdrawal from the group on one evening in particular and occasional intolerance were a clear measure of my lack of success. I have had to relearn this lesson — that there are only unhappy consequences for me and others when I attempt to imprint my views or feelings on people who are in no mood to be imprinted — a thousand times during the course of my life. Perhaps we all do.

Parents and anybody else involved in the rearing of children have the toughest time of all. Because adults are in a position of authority, both their conscious and unconscious behaviour, moods, and words are easily imprinted on children — with long-term, even lifelong, effects. This is the meaning of the biblical observation that the sins of the fathers shall be visited upon the children even unto the third and fourth generations. It's why child abusers tend to produce child

The community in which we lived will make a very good biographer.

It seems to me that the quality of our life should concern us far more than the wake or trail we leave behind. If we endeavour to live well, to use our personal strengths effectively, and seek to be as healthy as we can be emotionally, our imprint will take care of itself.

Family

As I wander through the abandoned towns, peering into or entering one collapsing building after another, the scattered remnants of family life — a half-burned candle here, a small chest of drawers there, an upended bench, or a snatch of rotten cloth — cause me to imagine, again and again, the families that once called these houses "home."

All families are microcosms of the complex world in which we live. Here is where we first experience the shock of nastiness and the presence of evil, suffer from deprivation or overindulgence, have the opportunity to learn the value of balancing competition with cooperation, and feel the love of imperfect beings. A family is a training ground for life.

Whenever I think of the families long-departed from these towns and, indeed, of the very concept of family itself, it is children that always come first — and vividly — to mind. Perhaps it is because

our childhood is with us until we die, in more ways than we know or care to admit.

Several years ago, at Kolmanskop, I noticed two girls, about eight or nine years old, who were keen to explore some of the more dangerous buildings. The mother of one of the girls refused all of her daughter's requests and entreaties, until eventually the mother of the other girl said, "Come on, let's go with them." Since I was within hearing distance much of the time, I listened to the girls' exclamations of fear and wonder as they explored the spooky interiors. When they had departed, I found it easy to forgive them for all the imprints they had left in the sand, because these were not the footprints of casual sightseers, but of real explorers into history and their imaginations.

The two girls at Kolmanskop also gave me something to explore. Listening to their voices echoing through the buildings made me more aware than I had been that half a century of weathering had gradually transformed the original masculine appearance of certain rooms, characterized by hard lines and solid colours, into a more feminine rendering of delicate hues. Even the occasional wallpapers and decorative friezes that must have been *de rigueur* in Germany at the time the houses were built (Namibia was then German South West Africa) seemed to have a less formal and obvious appearance than they must have had originally. And this made me think of the mothers.

Because it is in a child's nature to be attracted by risky situations and experiences, which may destroy its innocence and naiveté, but

give its personality complexity and depth, a good mother will allow her child to take risks — to encounter both the good and the bad, even to flirt with danger — and then will affirm the child when it has acted in its own best interests, or comfort it when it has not.

Mothers can do this for their children in a way that many fathers cannot. What gets us through our risk-taking, what enables us to discover the experience of resurrection in our encounters with death is, as Thomas Moore puts it, "the profound maternal feeling in us for life, continuity, and fruitfulness . . . which paradoxically becomes more intense and more solidly established . . . when it is severely threatened." For me, the ocean mists that wash and cool the Namib, eventually stimulating, even far inland, the glowing blossoms of tiny succulents, are perfect symbols.

But what about fathers — both caring and uncaring ones? Most of the fathers in these desert towns, like fathers everywhere, probably were both physically and emotionally absent from their children often enough for the children to feel their absence keenly.

In *The Odyssey*, Homer really begins the story not with Odysseus, but with his son, Telemachus, who is missing his father terribly and longing for his return. Homer wants to plant the suggestion quickly that our experience of the father includes his absence and our longing for him.

Through his confusion, sadness, and longing, Telemachus evokes not only his "biological" father, but also "the father in himself," and

thus begins, as it must for each of us, the process of finding or developing the feelings of protection, authority, confidence, and wisdom, which means incorporating the experiences, good and bad, that life offers everybody who is willing to wander — both outside and inside themselves. Moore believes, as do I, that one becomes a father to one's own life by "becoming intimately acquainted with it and daring to traverse its waters." He's talking about "a deep father figure that settles into the soul to provide a sense of authority, the feeling that you are the author of your own life, . . . the head of the household in your own affairs."

All of us grow up to be fathers and mothers, if not to a new generation of children, then to ourselves. Or we should. But, in the process, we must never forget the child — the explorer — within us.

Doors and Windows

Doors and windows need walls. Without them they would not exist. And what is true of our physical constructions is equally true of our emotional ones. So, whenever we are thinking about doors and windows, physical or emotional, at some level we are also considering their context.

Doors that open to the outside of buildings, we usually keep closed. These doors make it easy for us, who live and work in the buildings, to come and go at will, but they also protect us and ensure our privacy. Not only do they keep other people and other creatures out, but they also keep the elements at bay — at least water (rain), earth (soil), and air (wind). Some doors are even effective against fire. Windows, on the other hand, are designed to let us see out and to let light — the most creative physical force in the universe — flood in.

This difference of purpose between doors and windows takes on special meaning when we think of a house as a symbol for one's self, which it is for most people. We identify with our houses, our

dwellings of whatever sort, and if we don't, we set about changing them — knocking down walls to open up interior space, or adding them to create new rooms, smaller and perhaps more intimate spaces. We raise or lower ceilings and windows, paint walls new colours, build shelves and closets, and choose new furniture — until we have finally transformed the house into a place where we feel at home. During this process and subsequently, we fill our dwellings, consciously and unconsciously, not only with what matters to us, but also with quite a lot that doesn't, which we euphemistically call "trash." Our houses, so to speak, are us.

In long-abandoned houses, doors often stand open and many of the windowpanes are missing, which gives the wind, soil, rain, and light the access that, previously, had been controlled by the people who lived there. Because these forces are continually altering the physical character and appearance of the interior, the symbol of the house as an expression of the self may be replaced by the symbol of the house as a loss-of-self. I wonder if this is why some people find abandoned buildings so threatening, and why many more experience such a sense of loss and sorrow. Is this why other people like to see old buildings "fixed up" or restored? It is never easy to deal with or accept the loss of self — at any level.

And what about me and the people like me who find derelict dwellings endlessly fascinating, who can't get enough of them? Why is our exploration never finished? What is our symbol?

This much I know. Every morning, as sunlight begins to stream through a certain window in Pomona, projecting a geometrical likeness of dusty and missing panes on the far wall, I want to be there. I want to observe the image moving imperceptibly down the wall as the angle of the light rises, then follow its slow, uneven trek across the sand that wind has heaped into the room, and continue to watch while the sun, rising ever higher above the window, contracts the broad image into a narrow band that, in the end, simply fades away. I like to sit for a while then, to live with the intensity of my feelings, to contemplate the beauty, the mystery, and, sometimes, the meaning of my experience.

This moving metaphor of my life cleanses my soul. In the space of an hour or so, I observe my beginning, my constant transition of form, always simple in its broad outlines, yet so full of complexities and rich with ambiguities, and finally my fading into unbroken shadow.

And this I also know. In Pomona there is a small house whose only west-facing window gathers the last warm rays of the setting sun into a little room. Here the brownish stucco walls reflect, bounce, and change the light until the whole interior of the room is glowing gold. When I stand in the shadow on the east side of the house, the shaded exterior wall is grey, except for where a panel missing from the door allows me to glimpse the radiant colour of the interior. Sometimes, it seems safe to say, the purpose of a window is to let the light shine out.

These two windows have caused me to regard all the abandoned

houses differently, to think of them not only as a symbol for the loss-of-self, but also as a powerful symbol for the giving-up-of-self, by which I mean the gradual process of self-acceptance. If we are lucky, well before we die we will have no secrets that cannot be shared, no doors and windows that we are afraid to leave open to the world, and thus no fear of living. Many of us find the journey to this place long and difficult, and our physical bodies, like the old towns of the southern Namib desert, show obvious signs of decay by the time we arrive.

Some people, of course, never undertake the journey. Among them, I think, are those who feel angry about my photographs of these relics in the sand, which are obviously functioning as symbols for them, as otherwise they would not be angry. For whatever reasons, they are afraid or unable to admit, even to themselves, the possible personal meanings of these symbols.

There are some interior doors in Kolmanskop through which the sand flows downward from a higher elevation into what I call "the blue room." For me, it has always been a place of surpassing beauty and peace. Perhaps there is no other reason for my reaction than the soothing effect of the colour, and that is fine with me. Perhaps it is because, here and there, the blue of the walls has been blasted away to reveal patches of the undercoat of white paint, which are so amorphous in their shapes that they take on the appearance of misty white clouds sailing through an azure sky. Although I am in a cool interior space, I feel as if I were a child lying in a meadow, staring at the midsummer

sky — oblivious to the fact that both the afternoon and the season, which shaped this reverie of innocence, will surely end.

There are some other doors in Kolmanskop through which the sand flows downward into a brown room. On one wall, larger than life, a 1920s bathing beauty kneels beside some curving lines that are meant to indicate water lapping on a beach — another reverie, one of desire and longing, but not of innocence. At least sixty years have passed since the songs of this Lorelei first lured sailors to their deaths by shipwreck.

Reveries. Dreams. Figments of my imagination. And, therefore, more real than reality. These episodic snippets from my journey evoke the big question. How can I participate as fully as possible in the experience of living? Collectively, these interior scenes of the houses repeat the symbolism of the morning light projecting the moving image of the window on the wall and the sand. In the process they answer the question of the towns' appeal for me, their drawing power, which is nothing less than the offer of an overview, the opportunity to see myself from a place outside of myself and outside of the normal constraints of time and space.

I, for one, cannot ignore the offer and lose the opportunity. Whether I'm inside or outside, I want the doors and windows open.

Metamorphoses

During the middle of my first morning in Elizabeth Bay, I disappeared into the vast, cavernous shell of what once was and still is the most imposing and beautiful public building in the town — the community social centre. Nobody who was living there during its heyday was ever privileged to watch the changing spectacle that I witnessed during the next five hours, or would have wanted to gaze on such a vision of the town's future.

Although an expanse of high ceiling and roof was completely missing, allowing sunlight to cascade down into a large entertainment hall now strewn with debris and studded with low shrubs, other large roof sections were partly intact. One of these formed a broad pattern of very long, narrow, parallel wooden slats alternating with equally long and narrow bands of sky. By midmorning, sunlight began to stream through the openings, creating continuously changing patterns of light and shadow on the walls and the sand-covered floor far below.

Two years after my last visit to the building, during which I spent many more hours in the great hall of light and shadow, the visual and emotional impact remains acute, perhaps because the patterns moving through the room replicated the pattern of our emotional lives with such a pristine sharpness. Visually we are able to appreciate light only because of shadow or darkness, and darkness because of light. The difference between them, the contrast, gives meaning to both. But what is true in a physical sense has even more potency in an emotional context, where, like the negative and positive poles or charges in a battery, they work together to produce creative energy. At a profoundly personal, perhaps instinctual level, we all carry this healing truth within us.

When the sun had descended to a point in the western sky where its rays no longer angled downward through the spaces between the roof slats, I left the building whose stark contrasts had functioned for me as powerful life symbols. The sand streets led me past rows of derelict houses that I had seen, yet had not seen, before. Everything was simultaneously familiar and unfamiliar, because now the crumbling exterior walls and empty rooms that I had viewed by morning light were illuminated on their "afternoon side."

First, I approached some walls, giant honeycombs really, whose mortar remained intact, but whose bricks had been blasted away by the erosive power of wind-driven sand. The missing bricks had been replaced by rectangles of bright blue sky, or sky and white clouds, mounted in roughly textured, light brown frames. The network of mortar was supporting air.

I wandered on, poking my head through window frames whose glass lay shattered on the ground below, stepping gingerly through doors that had blown open years earlier, and doubling back frequently to see ways that changing light was influencing the appearance of rooms and artifacts. (The best walks are never in a straight line.) In a room in one house stood a small, rusting, whitish stove, no longer attached to a pipe or chimney. Deprived of its intended function, it served now as an ornament of history. In another room, a remnant washstand still clung firmly — almost ferociously, I thought — to the wall.

A couple of houses farther along, in a building of no particular distinction when viewed from the outside, I entered a once-ordinary room that had been overpainted to an extraordinary degree of surrealism by decades of exposure to the elements. It was like stumbling into the middle of a long-lost Magritte. A rusting bedstead, springs still in place, seemed suspended in an ominously green and steel-blue sky, where a turbulent arrangement of clouds portended a storm. Yet, the balanced geometry of the bedstead

induced a feeling of stability, almost serenity, that bestowed a strange kind of beauty upon the prospect of enormous atmospheric change.

Sand piled high against a door prevented me from entering one of the other rooms. So I circled the house, and as I rounded the corner that indicated the sealed room, I noticed that two small, side-by-side panes were missing from the east window. However, since the openings were well above my eye level and there was nothing around to use for constructing a solid viewing stand, I passed by with only a cursory glance at the ceiling.

How many times in my life have I made a similar mistake? How many times have I subsequently recognized I'd even made a mistake? And how many times have I been given — and taken — the opportunity to rectify it?

The following afternoon I walked by the same window on my way to a distant building, when I suddenly realized that this time I had glimpsed more than the ceiling — a fragment of colour, a darker tone, perhaps — in a lower corner of one of the missing panes. Backtracking, I looked upwards again. Nothing! Yet, I couldn't shake the feeling of having caught a hint of something, something important, something I needed to see.

I scrabbled through a nearby heap of disintegrating bricks until I found half a dozen large enough and sound enough to arrange into a very wobbly viewing platform against the side of the building. Standing on tiptoe, I gazed through the opening for a very long moment at a

remarkably well-preserved *trompe l'oeil* of palm trees arching over a lake or lagoon, the whole scene covering the entire far wall. The painting reminded me more of the Mediterranean than of an oasis, as the water seemed to have no visible horizon, which caused me to feel a profound sense of longing, not just for water, shade, and a view with a distance, but also for what they represent — a longing for emotional refreshment, for a quiet place of contemplation, and for freedom.

Sometimes when the voice of the unconscious calls to us, we cannot resist its calling — the urge to do what we need to do. Who created this wall-sized painting as a way of expressing outwardly the inner cry for change? Given the practical cirumstances of her life (or was a man the creator?), was she responding the only way she could at the time — metaphorically?

Maybe somebody knows who the painter was, maybe nobody. But the contents of the imagery reveal the painter's needs, and the sheer size of the creation conveys the strength of the painter's longing. More than that, there is nothing we need to know.

But there is something I'd like to know. When the painter had to leave the house and the painting, was he, or was she, ever able to find a place in her soul that provided water, shade, and a view with unlimited distance?

Out of the Rubble

 **I** entered Elizabeth Bay for the first time on a day when a heavy ocean fog was rolling across the sand and swirling through crumbling walls and heaps of brick rubble. Two of the men in our small group, both excellent amateur photographers, compared the scene of destruction to Berlin after the blitz, then quickly closeted themselves, along with their food, water, and sleeping bags, in the only building that was still remotely inhabitable, closing the doors behind them. Neither made any pictures that day. Their strongly negative emotional reaction to the haunted, empty shells suggested to me that they feared something dark and ominous in themselves rather than in the town, something they were repressing. Over the years I've buried my own fears in similar ways often enough to make me alert to the symptoms.

Both were industrious, successful men who had reached a comfortable place in their lives. This trip was one way they were enjoying the fruits of their labours. Yet, as I contemplated their behaviour, I wondered if they were neglecting to plant new trees from

which to harvest future crops, if perhaps they had suffered such a blitz of their own after years of hard work and responsibility that they were unconsciously choosing to disregard the creative impulse that had carried them so far.

Even if my speculation was totally off the mark as far as these two men were concerned, "retirement syndrome" is a fairly common disease. To admit that we have reached a creative dead end is so difficult that we may either repress the knowledge altogether or, as sometimes happens, deliver an advance version of our own eulogy by boasting about our past accomplishments.

Whenever we are confronted symbolically with situations we do not want to consider and emotions we do not like to feel, and we close our eyes and our hearts to scenes of actual abandonment and destruction — in ourselves, our family, our community, or our wider environment — because it's painful for us to keep them open, we risk the death of our creative impulse, and thus increase the possibility that our lives will become relatively meaningless, mediocre, and dull. To me, that's death.

So, difficult though it may be, it seems essential to me that everybody, but especially older people, remain sensitive to the negative aspects of life, that we continue to accept the reality of fear, pain, and suffering in the world both inside and outside ourselves, so we will learn to celebrate life's positive pleasures and joys more fully and openly than ever before. There are times when the best thing we can

possibly do is to turn and face a pursuing monster in a dream, or analyse honestly our negative emotional response to a symbol — in order to discover the nature of and reason for the cancer that is destroying our creative selves. When we confront the monster, it becomes a "giver of gifts" by exposing what we have repressed. Then, if we can muster the courage to change, if we can endure the agony of the surgery necessary for excising the diseased cells, our creative impulse will be resurrected, and we will be reborn into a new and dynamic existence. Or, as the philosopher and theologian Martin Buber so accurately describes the experience: "Everything depends on the inner change; when this has taken place, and only then, does the world change."

The morning after our arrival in Elizabeth Bay, accompanied by the slow drumbeat of a distant surf, the scarlet orb of the sun rose slowly, triumphantly, out of faraway dunes into the silver dome that arched above the entire visible world. Around me the hard-edged silhouettes of broken walls softened. Doorways began to open, revealing corridors of light. Enormous Mondrians materialized. The blitz was over, and out of the rubble a new world was being created.

Beckoned by the light, all the photographers emerged — some earlier, some later — each embarking on a personal exploration. Nature is forever repairing, rebuilding, and creating. And each of us, being creations of nature, or "creatures," also experience the urge, at some level and to some degree, to be creators as well.

Nature and Human Nature

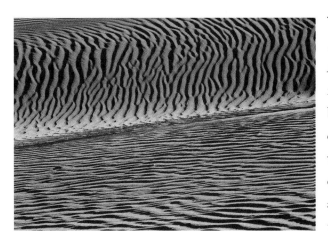

No desert is barren. Anybody who refers to "the barren desert" either hasn't visited a desert or wasn't paying attention when they did.

Because of their varying geological histories, their topographies, and a host of other natural conditions and circumstances, deserts are filled with living things. The world's oldest living plant, *Welwitschia mirabilis*, makes the Namib its home, and even though many desert plants are small, the *Welwitschia* isn't. *Lithops* and other related small succulents, often referred to as "stone plants" (because they resemble stones), live here too. Many other succulents, large and small, a wide range of shrubs, numerous grass species, and even trees occupy niches in the desert ecosystems. Animals — insects, reptiles, birds, and

mammals — vary as much as plants in the ways that they have adapted to arid and semi-arid conditions.

And no desert is barren aesthetically. The Namib's night music of animal sounds — wonderful choirs, whose choruses are usually punctuated by cries and calls and chirps — gives way to profoundly cleansing silence. But the wind plays its own symphonies when it chooses — night or day. Fields of marble and grains of quartz shimmer in the slanting light of morning and afternoon; rippled surface patterns of sweeping, curvaceous dunes may bear the undulating tracery of a sand adder or be punctuated by the emerging orb of a long-buried ostrich egg; and deep, rocky canyons lure the wandering spirit. In a desert, a person's emotions float to the surface — at least mine do, and especially in the Namib.

So, I feel, did those of August Stauch, when he arrived in 1907 to supervise a short section of the railway line that ran east from the port of Lüderitz (mainly to keep it cleared of low, rapidly moving dunes). This young man, who had to leave his wife and children behind in Germany and did not see them again for two years, quickly developed a fascination with the natural history of the desert. Part of his interest was a geological one and, within a year, he had discovered the first diamonds in that part of Africa, setting off the great diamond rush that, in a highly modified and controlled way, continues to this day.

Stauch's interest in the natural history and aesthetics of the desert was soon subsumed in his pursuit of diamonds, and the new purpose behind his excursions into the desert was to stake claims. It was only as an older man living in Germany again, after twenty years of gaining incredible wealth and eventually losing it in the period between the two world wars, that he focused his attention once more on the natural realm — almost to the point of desperation.

Whether or not Jesus' questions "For what will it profit a man, if he gains the whole world and forfeits his life? Or what shall a man give in return for his life?" can be reasonably asked about August Stauch, I do not know, but his final dissatisfactions with life and the nature of human behaviour raise these questions in my mind.

Stauch is gone, and the towns of the diamond fields are going as well. Nature is instinctively endeavouring to reclaim the desert. Yet, despite all the guidance that nature offers us, our so-called self-interest remains paramount and fights the reclamation. We still regard deserts and all other types of ecosystems — marshlands, grasslands, forests, and oceans — primarily as sources of materials that we can exploit for perceived human good and pleasure. Although we know that the well-being of the planet, which also means our own well-being, depends fundamentally on our taking only what we need, and needing what we take, we have yet to admit that deserts usually are ecologically fragile but dynamic communities (or groups of communities) that function best when they are left to their own interactions, which for thousands of years included very small human populations that were essentially non-exploitive.

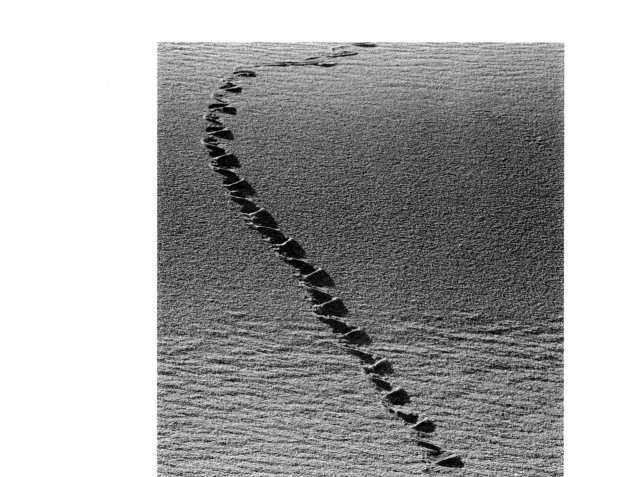

Personally, I experience enormous anguish when I see roads being built or transmission towers being erected without the slightest concern for ecology or natural aesthetics. There are places in the Namib — and elsewhere — to which I refuse to return because of the human destruction. But I know that, one day, these, too, will be gone. And perhaps more quickly than anybody expects. Whether or not our species must first disappear is a question that will never be answered for me, but in a way it doesn't matter. From nature's standpoint, we are no more special than the species we are extinguishing every day and, like every other individual and every other species, we have a limited life span. So, I am able to imagine deserts of the future with a sense of relief and a feeling of joy.

Cracks in the Walls

In the towns of the Forbidden Territory, I see my own face in the weathered walls of deeply cracked and peeling paint. They are the mirror of my future, and the future is arriving.

We are taught to dread wrinkles. By the time we are adolescents, we have learned to regard them as undesirable, unnatural, and therefore certainly not inevitable. How else could the entire anti-aging industry have been built — an industry that subtly exploits our none-too-subliminal fear of dying?

Wrinkles keep millions of people "gainfully" employed developing, marketing, and selling skin lotions and cosmetics. They have a huge (and hugely successful) impact on the fashion industry, and account for a major segment of the advertising industry. Wrinkles support (and sometimes line the pockets of) plastic surgeons and psychiatrists. They even assist in maintaining the numerical strength and financial health of the many religious groups whose main enterprise is offering the ultimate cosmetic — life everlasting — to people who feel unable or unwilling to cope with the cracks and wrinkles they encounter in their lives on Earth.

My mother never became a victim of the anti-wrinkle lobby. She accepted her wrinkles as being so natural that she never mentioned them. As she grew older and more at peace with herself, and thus with the world, her wrinkles became part of her beauty. And I, not strangely at all, didn't really notice them, but saw instead her wonderfully textured countenance. Maybe that's why I'm attracted by the weathered walls of the Namibian ghost towns. I don't see the individual lines so much as the overall appearance of texture, which is often very beautiful.

When it rains in this part of Africa, pools of water accumulate where clays form the surface layer of the soil. Then, as the ravenous winds and the sun's heat suck the moisture from the land, even from the soil itself, cracks forming on the surface deepen and spread into network patterns of lines and shapes.

Viewed close up, the overall patterns disintegrate. Instead, one sees the individual lines and shapes. Viewed from a distance, especially from a hilltop, the networks re-form and tighten, taking on

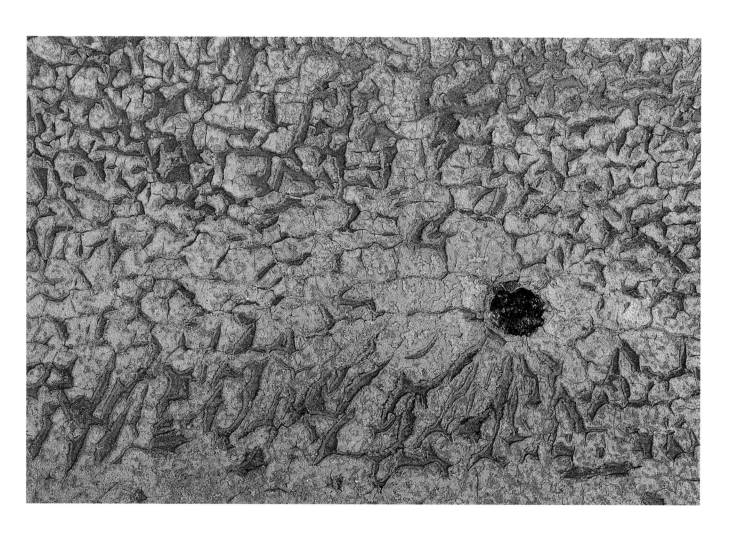

the appearance of a fabric. Textures, which can best be described as the weave or fabric-like nature of surfaces, are something of an illusion, a creation of space and distance. But that doesn't make them any less real.

Perhaps it was the weathered walls of the abandoned houses, or the patterns of dried mud in the desert, or my mother's wrinkles, or my own — or more likely all of these things and more — that made me realize that textures are also a creation of time, that they develop, grow, spread, and change. One line, one shape, one experience, or even several of each do not make a texture. The creation of texture requires an accumulation of shapes, lines, or experiences.

Our lives provide the space and the opportunities for such an accumulation. Although each of us is given the opportunity to participate in the creation of our own personal fabric, none of us is compelled to do so. For those who choose to be active participants, the rewards can be very satisfying. Recently, a friend who was celebrating his fiftieth birthday remarked, "I find life so rich now." His comment brought tears to my eyes, but it did not surprise me. Because he has given his creative best for most of his life, he is filled with experiences and surrounded by friends, each one forming a strand in the richly textured fabric of his life.

In a way that has nothing to do with money, growing older can be synonymous with growing richer.

Mortal Remains

Many people, seeing for the first time the ghost towns of Namibia, think of death. The decay is so palpable, the sense of human beings having come and gone irrevocably is so strong, that it is difficult not to think of mortality, including one's own.

On a hilltop beyond Pomona there is a cemetery overlooking the ocean. The view is dramatic, the location suggesting that the dead can see, and that this site was selected in order to satisfy a longing in all those who would be buried there — the longing for water.

In a little valley below the cemetery, on the side away from the sea, there is a scattering of empty wine bottles, partly exposed to the air or partly covered by the sand — depending on one's point

of view. Why are they there? Is their story partly revealed or partly hidden?

In the cemetery, one grave has been ripped open. There is a ragged hole in the centre. I do not know whether it was made from above or from below. I met somebody near the grave. Neither a woman nor a man, or perhaps both. I wanted to ask a question.

Does thirst survive death?

In the morning the ocean is blue; in the evening it is silver, or gold, or scarlet. Some days it is grey. Other days a cold, white mist hangs over the cemetery and hides the ocean from both the dead and the living. One day I wanted to ask a question about this, but I didn't meet anybody, so I asked myself.

Do I need a body in order to see?

I do not believe in heaven, at least not as a place of unending bliss. My father used to say, "People can't stand prosperity," and he was right. If everything were perfect, and therefore static, creativity would be dead. That's why the universe never allows for perfection. And that's why I don't believe in eternal joy and happiness. I don't even want it. I want to keep on being thirsty, and hungry too.

But I wonder about "the body."

The people of many ancient cultures buried their dead with food and drink, so they believed in the continued existence of the sentient body. I don't.

Once, science was considered to be an antidote to old

"superstitions," but what it has taken away it has given back by providing bases for new understandings that are often quite harmonious with other traditional beliefs — especially those that have recognized the fundamental unity of nature and regarded human beings as part of the natural world, or acknowledged mystical connections between the living and the dead. And this strong movement on the part of modern science toward early religious understandings continues, perhaps because both are characterized by a desire for knowing, rather than by blind faith.

It is a simple scientific fact that I am always dying and being reborn, continuously shedding body cells in order to provide space for their successors. The atoms that make up the cells of my body have been around from the beginning, and they change places all the time. I trade atoms continuously with water and sand, flowers and ferns, foxes and falcons, airplanes, motorcycles, and cardboard boxes. At this very moment I may possess atoms that once inhabited blue-green algae, dinosaurs, a Bronze Age hatchet, and emperors of China. So I will certainly live on in atomic form.

And will I survive like water in the sea — my experience absorbed by and functioning without individuation in the collective psychological inheritance of mankind? I can say "Yes" to that as well. The scientific evidence is quite firm. But will "I" survive — the unique self who is always changing physically, mentally, and emotionally, yet always remaining the same? I don't think so.

By accepting the fact of my eventual death I am able to cherish

life more. There is an incredible sweetness to close friendships, for example. And because I don't postpone anything for "the hereafter," lilacs seem to become more fragrant with every passing spring, the complex and savoury freshness of a great salad lingers on my tongue and in my memory longer than ever before, and exquisite music fills my house in the middle of the night.

Also, by accepting the impending loss of my unique self, I know that one day I will finally be abandoning hubris, which the universe or "God-by-any-other-name" demands of each of us. This makes it easier for me now to keep my accomplishments and contributions, such as they are, in perspective.

When visitors to Pomona cemetery lift their eyes from the graves to gaze upon the ocean, will they remember that their ancestors have departed, physical atom by physical atom, into that vast and turbulent mix? Will they regard the sea as a symbol for that other ocean where the dead live on — the collective unconscious? Will they, like me, ask if it is enough? And what will they answer?

Departures

I leave the towns with a feeling of wanting to stay. And yet there comes a time, every time, when I feel satiated. Because of the prolonged intensity of my emotional reactions, the symbols begin to weaken for me. A person can enjoy only so much rich food, or make love for only so long. When I realize that I have exhausted my potential for seeing more or seeing better — this time — I have to go away and live my "normal" life again. If I am able to carry the experiences of the towns — my heightened feelings and my new perceptions — with me into the realm of everyday existence, I will be able to return to the towns one day with a strong desire to know them, and myself, better still.

Everybody has a built-in resistance to living at one pole — whether the positive or the negative — for an extended period. We become inured to the hell of unbroken suffering and bored by the heaven of unending peace, because both are static conditions, and so we seek change and potential growth in the uncertainty and the struggle of the creative middle, where things are always happening. Perhaps, a place called Earth.

Our search for the creative centre is utterly natural in a universe formed by the creating and harmonizing of differences — a dynamic universe. It is here that the balancing of opposites occurs — without the opposites being destroyed. The ecological truism that all wet places tend to become dry and all dry places tend to become wet illustrates both the movement toward the centre and the preservation of the differences. A healthy human relationship, of course, is the emotional arena where differences are recognized, confronted, struggled with, and harmonized.

The towns of Die Sperrgebiet make the same point in another way. They were built by flawed human beings, like me, who, on the one hand, represented the ideal of "the good life" in the size and ornate beauty of some of their buildings, but who, on the other hand, expressed their emotional dissatisfaction and restlessness with equal clarity — through the *trompe l'oeil* in Elizabeth Bay, the sketch of the bathing beauty in Kolmanskop, and the piles of empty beer bottles here and there. Although it was realities mainly beyond their own control that caused everybody to leave, could any of the towns have survived their internal contradictions to become enduring healthy and functioning communities?

There can never be a final answer to a question like this. The only success we can claim is our present success. Tomorrow we may

be back in a struggle. But, since we can learn from our experiences, both good and bad, we can have a reasonable hope of achieving a new success, and another new one after that. We can build.

For me, the approaching end of a visit to the abandoned towns of the Namib is a period of creative withdrawal. As I explore the metaphors and symbols of individual and collective life that the towns provide, I am keenly aware of the fact that I will soon be leaving. Must leave, in fact, just like the diamond workers, managers, and families over half a century ago. Except for the fact of change itself, everything and everybody is continuously changing in some way; the only certainty we have is uncertainty. This is often very difficult to accept and to bear.

Yet, when we choose to engage life actively, to live creatively, however painful this may be at times, we are welcoming a departure as the beginning of a new odyssey.

NOTES ON PHOTOGRAPHS

Frontispiece
p. ii   Interior of a house, Kolmanskop

Introduction
p. 1   A pair of discarded gumboots, Bogenfels
p. 3   Early-morning light streaming across sand inside a house, Kolmanskop
p. 4   Early-morning light illuminating rooms and doorways, Kolmanskop
p. 7   Two interior doorways, Pomona

Approaches
p. 8   Sand filling a small room, Pomona
p. 9   Elizabeth Bay from a distance
p. 12   An unidentified figure resting in the remains of a stuffed chair, Bogenfels
p. 13   The frontal view of "the grande dame of Bogenfels" on a misty morning

Imprints
p. 15   Clouds above the desert near Pomona
p. 16   An unidentified figure wandering in the desert near Pomona
p. 18   Remains of the narrow-gauge railway (essential for delivering water) that ran between the towns
p. 20   An abandoned bathtub in the sand, Kolmanskop
p. 21   A large expanse of cracked mud, Bogenfels
p. 23   Steps to a missing building, Kolmanskop

Family
p. 24   Bedsteads protruding from sand cascading into a bedroom, Pomona
p. 25   Remains of a wicker settee inside a house in Pomona
p. 26   Human and insect impressions on the sand inside "the grande dame of Bogenfels"
p. 28   A small chest being buried by a dune inside a Bogenfels house
p. 29   A chest of drawers in an otherwise empty room, Pomona
p. 31   The harmonious colours of sand, wall, and doorway in a Kolmanskop house
p. 33   An old sofa in the Kolmanskop community centre prior to the building's restoration

Doors and Windows
p. 34   The weathered door and frame of a Pomona house
p. 35   The geometrical likeness of a window projected on sand and a wall, Pomona
p. 37   The view through four doorways and five rooms of sand in a Kolmanskop house
p. 39   Sand cascading into "the blue room" of a Kolmanskop house
p. 40   Large wall sketch of a 1920s bathing beauty (entitled: Miss Colmass Koppa) adorning a room in Kolmanskop
p. 42   The exterior view of a wall, steps, and doorway on an overcast day in Pomona
p. 43   A glimpse through a missing door panel into a room illuminated by evening light

Metamorphoses

p. 45   A honeycomb pattern of mortar and missing bricks, Elizabeth Bay

p. 47   The interior of the great hall of "light and shadow" in the Elizabeth Bay community centre —
the sky showing through slats exposed by the missing roof

p. 48   Patterns of light and shadow created by roof slats in a Kolmanskop house

p. 49   Patterns of light on interior walls in the community centre, Elizabeth Bay

p. 51   A stove left behind in an Elizabeth Bay house

p. 52   A bedstead standing in front of a sand-blasted wall, Elizabeth Bay

p. 54   A *trompe l'oeil* of palm trees and water in an Elizabeth Bay house

Out of the Rubble

p. 56   A wall painting in an Elizabeth Bay house

p. 57   A cemented-up doorway that interrupts a weathered wall painting, Elizabeth Bay

p. 58   A misty-day impression of "the blitz" of Elizabeth Bay caused by wind, sand, and sea fog

p. 59   Morning light shining through the tiny window openings of a Pomona building

p. 61   An unidentified person peering through the window of a Kolmanskop hospital ward

p. 62   Light emanating from a house in Pomona

p. 63   Strange light illuminating a weathered interior wall in Kolmanskop

Nature and Human Nature

p. 65   Sand ripples on a dune to the west of the Klinghardt mountains, southern Namib

p. 66   Among the sand dunes to the west of the Klinghardt mountains, southern Namib

p. 69   The trail of a sand adder on a large dune near Pomona

p. 70   An ostrich egg protruding from the sand

Cracks in the Walls

p. 72   Cracked and peeling paint, Kolmanskop

p. 74   Peeling paint, Elizabeth Bay

p. 75   Pattern of cracked paint, Elizabeth Bay

Mortal Remains

p. 77   The setting sun, Elizabeth Bay

p. 78   An unidentified person in Pomona cemetery

p. 80   Empty shelves and rusty tin in the Pomona infirmary

p. 81   The main hall of the Pomona infirmary

p. 83   A wave crashing against rocks at Elizabeth Bay

Departures

p. 85   A sand-filled liquor bottle, Bogenfels

p. 87   The stage in the auditorium of the Kolmanskop community centre before the
building was restored. ("SEKT" is German for champagne.)

Back flap

The author in Pomona